A Love Letter to Myself

ESTHER COHEN

BALBOA.PRESS

A DIVISION OF HAY HOUSE

Balboa Press books may be ordered through booksellers or by contacting:

Balboa Press
A Division of Hay House
1663 Liberty Drive
Bloomington, IN 47403
www.balboapress.com
844-682-1282

Interior Graphics/Art Credit: Sharon Johnson

ISBN: 979-8-7652-3885-1 (sc)
ISBN: 979-8-7652-3886-8 (e)

Print information available on the last page.

Balboa Press rev. date: 02/16/2023

Everyday is harder not knowing when I will see you or hear from you.

The love we had was out of novel

I long for you.

Will I ever heal?

Time will tell when I will see you..

I will never forget this fairytale.

Tell me you love me.

Everyday is harder then the other.

Will destiny be kind and bring us together?

I wish I was strong like you to hold my urges.

I count the time and pray I speak to you again…

Time is still.

Will I ever heal?

Where am I going?

What will become of this love?

Will it be a fated memories?

You are forever in printed my heart.

My heart bleeds when I think of you.

You are the most special man I ever met.

This is what true love is.

I'm in heaven when I'm with you

But in hell when I'm not.

Will I ever love like this again?

Thinking of you always…

Are you thinking of me?

Do you feel pain like me?

Will I ever get over this?

Will you ever comeback and heal my heart?

You are my fairytale prince.

Is there a future between us?

I wonder this everyday…

Will you come to me and make me whole again?

Will we have a happy ever after?

All I know is that I love you so much that it hurts me everywhere.

All I want to do is contact you.

I know I'm not supposed to.

I need to give you space for you to come back to me.

when you are ready.

This is so hard.

I will give you my whole heart and soul because you deserve me.

Will you ever love me again?

This was a dream come true.

A love like this is once in a lifetime.

It was worth every second I spent with you.

I will cherish this forever.

My David...

You stole my heart the second I met you.

I never thought a love like this ever existed.

I saw the world in a different way the day I met you.

You made me a better person since I met you.

You are pure and innocent.

I want you to always be happy every second of your life.

Never ever forget you are my heart and soul.

For my best friend Sharon Johnson,

Nobody beats you.

You are the smartest, the strongest woman I ever met.

You are my inspiration.

I'm so lucky to have you as my best friend.

You are equally gorgeous inside and out.

You are always there for me. Without any judgement.

You are the most special person I ever met. Please never forget that.

I count my blessings everyday.

You were send out to from things.

I did not even know about.

I know GOD loves me because he sent me you are a human angel.

I just feel so much pain.

You said you did not want to hurt me.

Yes you hurt me more by ignoring me.

You said loved me and you were thinking of me.

So where are you when I need you the most?

I love you with all my heart.

I wish I could be more like you.

Not feel anything and be carefree.

This is really not easy for me.

Live and love that's all we have in life.

Best to spend it in the most positive way.

Never live in regret that is the biggest curse in life.

Time flies like sand in an hourglass.

I hate you.

I love you.

I hate you.

I love you.

Why can you just man up.

Stop being scared.

Life is too short.

You tell me you don't love.

I don't believe you.

I believe what I feel inside.

I know deep inside you are scared man.

The heart does not lie.

Neither does my intuition.

You were meant to love me.

As I was meant to love you.

Who are you fooling?

You can fool yourself.

You can't fool me.

The heart does not lie.

When we are young we read Cinderella and Snow White.

Growing up like that. Thinking you will meet your prince in a white horse who will save you from all of your sorrows.

As I have realized, aging it does not work like that.

Sometimes you have to be your own hero and loving yourself as a true hero would.

You are the man I love.

No matter what happens

You are imprinted in my heart.

Love you forever.

My heart bleeds when I think of you.

You are the most special man I ever met.

This is what true love is.

I'm in heaven when I'm with you

But in hell when I'm not.

Will I ever love like this again?

Will I forgive me?

Will I forgive you?

Will you not be scared anymore?

How long can this go on for?

Need back my heart,

healed in one piece.

Was it all on dream?

This connection?

Did I imagine it?

Or are you my one and only?

He loves me,

He loves me not,

What will it be?

I'm going out of my skin.

For Sibu,

The super hero I know...

Who came in our lives and saved the day.

You are a human angel.

Everyone who encounters you is truly blessed.

My heart is on fire when I think of you.

The memories never seem to go away.

The pain is still there like it was yesterday.

They say time heals.

Will it heal?

When I was with you, you made me feel like a queen.

When I'm not with you I'm in pain.

Hope you will come back to me very soon.

I know you are scared.

I love you with all my heart.

I wish I could be more like you.

Not feeling anything and being carefree

This is really not easy for me.

To my son David.

You completely changed my life the day I met you.

You are the most magnificent boy I ever met.

I hope you treat people well.

I hope you change the word in a positive way.

I hope achieve greatness.

Most of all I hope you will be happy and healthy.

Relationships

Block.

Unblock.

Modern day relationship.

What happened to romance?

I live for my son to be happy.

I live to be happy.

I live to love.

I live to smile

I live to shine.

He loves.

He loves me not

Time will tell..

Will this be the greatest relationship

Of all?

Or the worst pain?

Did I understand what you wrote?

Did you understand what I wrote.

Is this a whole misunderstanding?

I love you

Did you love me?

Will this be the only way we ever communicate?

What is love?

Love is giving not taking.

Love is sacrifice, respect.

Men are the givers.

Women are the receivers.

If you don't have that you don't have love.

Will I ever hear from you?

You said you love me and are thinking of me….

What is stopping you?

I'm not afraid.

Why are you?

To love is not to hurt.

To love is to feel butterflies.

To love is the feeling on endless joy.

To love is to smile.

To love your soulmate is a different level.

Loving yourself is not always easy.

You wish you can do things differently.

You wish you did not make so many mistakes.

All you can do is accept yourself love yourself and commit to be better.

For all women.

As women, we have so much pressure to be skinny.

To always look perfect.

To starve ourselves.

To exercise a lot.

These goals are impossible and extreme.

People die everyday and destroy their lives from eating disorders.

The recovery of these diseases are a huge nightmare.

We must change the image that we see of women.

Love ourselves and appreciate ourselves

We are all beautiful!!

You are the man I love.

No matter what happens

You are imprinted in my heart.

Love you forever.

To love?

Or not love?

Love is the best feeling of pure joy in the world.

Not loving is truly feeling your soul emptying

one day at a time.

I live in regret.

Wish I would have done so many things differently.

Wish I did not make so many mistakes.

Wish I did not hurt anyone.

Wish I knew then what I know now.

This one of the hardest things.

Will the pain ever stop?

Will my heart heal?

Will I ever be truly happy like I was with you?

All I can do is wait and dream that one day our paths will cross again.

Time is still.

Will I ever heal?

Where am I going?

What will become of this love?

Will it be a fated memories?

You are forever in printed my heart.

My son David is my world.

He is the best thing that has ever happened to me.

He is my reason for everything.

I hope he will grow up and be very happy.

I love him with all my heart and my soul.

Is there a future between us?

I wonder this everyday…

Will you come to me and make me whole again?

Will we have a happy ever after?

Only time will tell …

All I know is that

I love you so much that it hurts me everywhere.

Will you ever love me again?

This was a dream come true.

A love like this is once in a lifetime.

It was worth every second I spent with you.

I will cherish this forever.

Where are you?

Will you reach out to me?

Are you thinking of me?

Time is going by so quickly.

My pain is still here.

Will I ever hear from you?

You said you love me and are thinking of me….

What is stopping you?

I'm not afraid.

Why are you?

What is love?

Love is living.

Love is feeling reborn.

Love is giving.

Love is the best reason to be alive.

I miss us

Will it ever be?

Will it be a blurry memory?

Or will be a dream come true?

Where are you when I need you?

I once thought we would walk down the aisle.

The best love I ever had.

I'm still thinking of you

Are you still loving me?

Tell me you love me.

How long can this go on for?

You brought so much joy in my life.

Will you ever comeback?

To marry or not to marry?

That's the man I love fear.

What's worse is living in pain?

Living with the what ifs

I gave you my heart.

You gave me yours.

We loved each other.

Then it all stopped.

When I think of you, my heart starts racing,
butterflies in my stomach.
I always think what is going on with you…
How is it so easy for you?

Will this nightmare end?

Will you not be so scared anymore?

Will you ever reach out to me again?

Can this story continue?

Will this pain go away?

Will this love continue?

Even if we are not together now.

I will love you forever.

You saw my soul.

I saw your soul.

I'm perfect in your eyes.

You are perfect in my eyes.

I love you.

I miss you.

What do I do?

This pain is so difficult.

My love for you gets stronger for you everyday.

Not sure what will become of this.

Time will tell...

If this nightmare will continue or stop.

David, my son

My loves grows for you everyday.

Everyday you make me smile

Everyday you make laugh.

You are my reason to be happy.

I'm truly blessed with you.

I love you more then air.

I love helping people.

Making the world a better place.

That is what we are here for.

Giving always feels better then getting.

Time is going by…

I still haven't heard from you.

What is taking you so long..

Do you still love me?

Broken heart.

Broken love.

Why does everything brake?

Why can't things just stay together?

I loved you with all my heart and soul.

You loved me with all your heart and soul.

Something told me you were scared.

Then it was over.

We all live once...

Why bother and be scared?

It's waste of time.

Love like there is no tomorrow.

My son David.

You make me the happiest mother in the world.

You are perfect.

You are the smartest boy I ever met.

You are the funniest boy.

You are way beyond my expectations.

I love you more then oxygen.

Life is love.

Love is life.

Without we are empty.

Love is the fuel that keeps us going.

I love you.

You love me.

Let's not give up.

Because we deserve it.

We fell in love.

It was not hard.

Something changed.

Then the world stopped.

About the Author

The Author speaks very simply about her life experiences. She sees life through empathetic eyes, in almost a childlike manner. She understands that a few words may go a long way. Her readers' may gain a sense of her almost philosophical mannerisms through a very brief sketch like expressionist way with wordings.

Through sadness, love, brokenness and pain; the author paints for us a picture of her own personal struggle through doubt and instability that life can be lived not only through pain but through the experiencing of struggles, doubts and insecurities a person can build a higher consciousness of oneself and, through her eyes therefore experience a sense of positivity and self love and how this can both quiet and quell many of those personal insecurities.

She believes that love and as she has learned "self love"is not easily achieved but is learned through trial and error, travails, and experiences is what makes life truly rich.

Printed in the United States
by Baker & Taylor Publisher Services